HIP-HOP STARS

LL COOL J

HIP-HOP STARS

Beastie Boys
Sean Combs
Missy Elliott
Eminem
Jay-Z   **LL Cool J**
          Queen Latifah
            Run-DMC
          Tupac Shakur
        Russell Simmons

HIP-HOP STARS

LL COOL J

Dustin Shekell

CHELSEA HOUSE
PUBLISHERS
An imprint of Infobase Publishing

LL COOL J

Chelsea House
An imprint of Infobase Publishing
132 West 31st Street
New York, NY 10001

Library of Congress Cataloging-in-Publication Data

Shekell, Dustin.
  LL Cool J / Dustin Shekell.
    p. cm. — (Hip-hop stars)
  Includes bibliographical references (p.   ), discography (p.   ), and index.
  ISBN-13: 978-0-7910-9519-5 (hardcover)
  ISBN-10: 0-7910-9519-3 (hardcover)
  1. L. L. Cool J, 1968—Juvenile literature. 2. Rap musicians—United States—Biography—Juvenile literature. I. Title. II. Series.

  ML3930.L115S54 2007
  782.421649092—dc22   2007000902

Text design by Erik Lindstrom
Cover design by Ben Peterson

Printed in the United States of America

Bang NMSG 10 9 8 7 6 5 4 3 2 1

This book is printed on acid-free paper.

CONTENTS

INTRODUCTION
By Chuck D

Hip-Hop: A Brief History

Like the air we breathe, hip-hop seems to be everywhere. The lifestyle that many thought would be a passing fad has, three decades later, grown to become a permanent part of world culture. Hip-hop artists have become some of today's heroes, replacing the comic book worship of decades past and joining athletes and movie stars as the people kids dream of being. Names like 50 Cent, P. Diddy, Russell Simmons, Jay-Z, Foxy Brown, Snoop Dogg, and Flavor Flav now ring as familiar as Elvis, Babe Ruth, Marilyn Monroe, and Charlie Chaplin.

While the general public knows many of the names, videos, and songs branded by the big companies that make them popular, it's also important to know the holy trinity, the founding fathers of hip-hop: Kool DJ Herc, Grandmaster Flash, and

Afrika Bambaataa. All are deejays who played and presented the records that rappers and dancers delighted themselves upon. Bambaataa single-handedly stopped the gang wars in the 1970s with the themes of peace, unity, love, and having fun.

Hip-hop is simply a term for a form of artistic creativity that was spawned in New York City—more precisely, the Bronx—in the early to mid-1970s. Amidst the urban decay in the areas where black and Hispanic people dwelled, economic, educational, and environmental resources were depleted. Jobs and businesses were all but moved away. Living conditions were of a lower standard than the rest of the city and country. Last but not least, art and sports programs in the schools were the first to be cut for the sake of lowering budgets; thus, music classes teaching the subject's history and techniques were all but lost.

From these ashes, like a phoenix, rose an art form. Through the love of technology and records found in family collections or even those tossed out on the street, the deejay emerged. Different from the ones heard on the radio, these folk were innovating a style that was popular on the island of Jamaica. Two turntables kept the music continuous, with the occasional voice on top of the records. This was the very humble beginning of rap music.

Rap music is actually two distinct words: rap and music. "Rap" is the vocal application that is used on top of the music. On a vocal spectrum, it is between talking and singing and is one of the few alternatives for vocalizing to emerge in the past 50 years. It's important to know that inventors and artists are side by side in the importance of music's development. Let's remember that inventor Thomas A. Edison created the first recording, with "Mary Had a Little Lamb" in 1878, most likely in New Jersey, the same state where the first rap recording—Sugarhill Gang's "Rappers Delight"— was made more than 100 years later, in 1979.

It's hard to separate the importance of history, science, language arts, and education when discussing music. Because of the social silencing of black people in the United States from slavery in the 1600s to civil rights in the 1960s, much sentiment, dialogue, and soul is wrapped within the cultural expression of music. In eighteenth-century New Orleans, slaves gathered on Sundays in Congo Square to socialize and play music. Within this captivity many dialects, customs, and styles combined with instrumentation, vocals, and rhythm to form a musical signal or code of preservation. These are the foundations of jazz and the blues. Likewise, it's impossible to separate hip-hop and rap music from the creativity of the past. Look within the expression and words of black music and you'll get a reflection of history itself. The four creative elements of hip-hop—emceeing (the art of vocalization); deejaying (the musician-like manipulation of records); break dancing (the body expression of the music); and graffiti (the drawn graphic expression of the culture)—have been intertwined in the community before and since slavery.

However, just because these expressions were introduced by the black–Hispanic underclass, doesn't mean that others cannot create or appreciate hip-hop. Hip-hop is a cultural language used best to unite the human family all around the world. To peep the global explosion, one need not search far. Starting just north of the U.S. border, Canadian hip-hop has featured indigenous rappers who are infusing different language and dialect flows into their work, from Alaskan Eskimo to French flowing cats from Montreal and the rest of the Quebec's provincial region. Few know that France for many years has been the second largest hip-hop nation, measured not just by high sales numbers, but also by a very political philosophy. Hip-hop has been alive and present since the mid-1980s in Japan and other Asian countries. Australia has been a hotbed in welcoming world rap acts, and it has also created its own vibrant hip-hop scene, with the reminder of its government's takeover of indigenous people reflected in every rapper's flow and rhyme. As a rhythm of the people, the continents of Africa and South America (especially Ghana, Senegal, and South Africa, Brazil, Surinam, and Argentina) have long mixed traditional homage into the new beats and rhyme of this millennium.

Hip-hop has been used to help Brazilian kids learn English when school systems failed to bridge the difficult language gap of Portuguese and patois to American English. It has entertained and enlightened youth, and has engaged political discussion in society, continuing the tradition of the African griots (storytellers) and folk singers.

For the past 25 years, hip-hop has been bought, sold, followed, loved, hated, praised, and blamed. History has shown that other cultural music forms in the United States have been just as misunderstood and held under public scrutiny. The history of the people who originated the art form can be found in the music itself. The timeline of recorded rap music spans more than a quarter century, and that is history in itself.

Presidents, kings, queens, fame, famine, infamy, from the great wall of China to the Berlin wall, food, drugs, cars, hate, and love have been rhymed and scratched. This gives plenty reason for social study. And I don't know what can be more fun than learning the history of something so relevant to young minds and souls as music.

Elder
Statesman

James Todd Smith. LL Cool J. Ladies Love Cool James. Uncle L. One man with many names. A man of unlimited ambition and the talent to back it up. A man of undeniable influence who helped introduce the music of the urban underground into suburban homes across the country.

LL Cool J has done what most rap artists have not been able to: He has remained relevant for more than two decades. As a pioneer of the genre, he has evolved along with the constantly changing hip-hop culture and has remained a superstar. Despite a career marked by controversy and criticism from his peers, LL has continually shifted gears and reinvented his image and his music to stay at or near the top.

With a career spanning more than two decades, LL Cool J continues to influence and contribute to the hip-hop community. Rap artist, movie star, television actor, author, and fashion director, LL Cool J has done it all. In an industry known for its one-hit wonders and short-lived careers, LL Cool J has proved himself to be an exception to the rule.

His eight consecutive platinum albums are a testament to his staying power and his 20+ movies and hit TV series prove that his star power extends far beyond music. In a youth-dominated industry filled with one-hit wonders and short-lived careers, Uncle L, one of rap's very few elder statesmen, continues to make music and be a vital part of hip-hop history well into his thirties.

HOW IT ALL BEGAN

The origins of rap music and the hip-hop culture can be traced back to three DJs from the Bronx: Kool Herc, Afrika Bambaataa, and Grandmaster Flash. Clive Campbell, a.k.a. Kool DJ Herc, was a Jamaican-born teenager trying to make a name for himself as one of his neighborhood's best DJs during late 1973. He was a master at finding the most danceable part of a reggae, funk, or soul record—known as the break—and playing it over and over to keep the crowd moving to the beat. Switching back and forth between two records, Herc routinely turned a "five second breakdown into a five-minute loop of fury," says hip-hop journalist and author Jeff Chang in his book *Can't Stop Won't Stop.*

More than anything, what separated Herc from other DJs in his neighborhood was the monstrously powerful sound system his father had lent him to perform at house and block parties. Not only was it the hugest and loudest system in the area but also it allowed Herc to hook up a microphone and talk and rhyme while he played records. Within a few years, Herc was the most popular DJ in the Bronx and was influencing other DJs, including Afrika Bambaataa and Grandmaster Flash, both of whom ushered hip-hop into the late 1970s and early 1980s.

As an art form, hip-hop has come a long way from its humble beginnings at a back-to-school party in a recreation room on Sedgwick Avenue in the Bronx, where Herc first became famous. LL Cool J and other rappers sell out arenas around the world. Hip-hop is not only a multimillion-dollar business

Clive Campbell, better known as DJ Kool Herc, is regarded as a pioneer of hip-hop music. The father of the breakbeat, DJ Kool Herc popularized the hip-hop tradition of isolating and repeating the most dance-able part of the song, "the break." During the 1970s, DJ Kool Herc was one of the most popular DJs in the Bronx, directly influencing DJs Africa Bambaata and Grandmaster Flash.

Hip-hop is not just a genre of music, it is a culture and a way of life. Hip-hop is represented in fashion, art, music, and dance. Break dancing is a major part of the hip-hop culture. In the photograph above, a B-boy stands on his head, a signature break dancing move.

but also the voice of an entire generation. Hip-hop's pervasive influence is abundantly evident, from urban youths listening to Jay-Z on street corners to suburban moms blasting Outkast through their minivan speakers.

Hip-hop began as a culture of young men and women searching for a way to express themselves in the urban sprawl

Inspired by the emerging hip-hop movement, LL Cool J began writing rhymes when he was just nine years old. Now in his thirties, LL Cool J has produced eight consecutive platinum-selling albums, won two Grammy Awards, and helped bring hip-hop to the forefront of pop culture.

of New York City. Like any culture, hip-hop was defined by the art, music, and self-expression of its people. Their paint-brushes were spray cans and markers. Their canvas was any surface available, from the walls of a subway station to the subway trains themselves, that would proudly display their illicit art form. Their dance floor was any piece of cardboard, linoleum, or smooth surface where the break-dancers, or B-boys, could show their head spins, gravity-defying acrobatics, and seemingly bone-bending popping skills. The foundation of the culture, however, and the glue that held it all together was rap music.

"Hip-hop is the only genre of music that allows us to talk about almost anything," Grandmaster Flash wrote in the fore-word of the *The Vibe History of Hip Hop.* "Musically it allows us to sample and play and create poetry to the beat of music."

INFLUENCING A NEW GENERATION

The early days of hip-hop inspired countless young people growing up in New York and gave them a way to express their creativity. One of those young people was a skinny, energetic boy named James Todd Smith. Armed with a quick wit and a gift for writing lyrics, Todd started writing rhymes when he was nine years old and has never stopped. Thanks to a life-changing present given to him by the most important man in his life, his grandfather, Todd went from rapping in front of his bedroom mirror to stealing the show at block parties to record-ing rap's first gold record—all before the age of 17. Known for his trademark Kangol hats and rolling up one pant leg to his knee, LL became hip-hop's new-school pioneer, pushing the culture to a never-before-seen level of national prominence.

However, before he became LL Cool J, Todd suffered through a childhood filled with abuse, violence, and instabil-ity. In his autobiography titled *I Make My Own Rules,* LL talks about how rap music gave him hope during a hopeless time:

I got deeper and deeper into it—and it got deeper and deeper into me. I was just hypnotized. There was power in this rap music, and it put me under a spell I've never come out of. Rap spoke to me, and in it I found myself and the power of my voice. Rap music was my escape from a living hell.

The Early Years

On January 14, 1968, in Bayshore, Long Island, New York, a hip-hop legend was born. Long before the world would know him as LL Cool J, James Todd Smith began his life with feuding parents and a paralyzed right arm. One of James and Ondrea Smith's worst fights started at a party when Ondrea was nine months pregnant with the only child they would ever have. According to Todd, as those close to LL call him, his father thought his wife was flirting with another man, and his jealousy lead to a public confrontation. The fight continued as James drove them home in their new 225 Buick. Steering the car with his left hand, James used his right hand to slap Ondrea's face repeatedly. Even though they were traveling at 30 miles per hour, Ondrea opened the door and jumped out of the car to escape.

LL Cool J, born James Todd Smith, endured a violent upbringing. When Todd was just four years old, his father shot Todd's mother and grandfather; fortunately, both survived the attack. The violence continued when his mother started dating a man who physically abused Todd for four years, until his mother found out about the beatings and left her boyfriend. Above, LL Cool J is photographed with his mother, Ondrea, at the 1996 MTV Video Music Awards.

This incident, just a few weeks before Todd's birth, may have contributed to the nerve damage that paralyzed Todd's right arm. With his mother's help, within a few months, Todd was able to lift his arm above his head. Within a year, it was just as functional as his left arm.

The relationship between Todd's parents didn't get any better as time went on, even though they seemed to be living the American Dream. Less than a year after Todd's birth, the Smiths moved into a house on Long Island with a big front yard and enough space to entertain guests. They had family and friends over all the time, especially during the summer, when James cooked hot dogs and burgers in the backyard barbeque pit. Every Fourth of July, he and his friends cooked an entire pig in the pit. On the outside, the Smiths might have looked like a happy family, with a new house, a young son, and an adorable little mutt they named Pup. Behind closed doors, LL said, things never improved between his parents. "They would fight over the dumbest things . . . and there I am right in the middle."

By the time Todd was four years old, Ondrea had had enough of James's verbal and physical abuse and decided to move out. She and Todd moved to her parents' house in St. Albans, Queens, New York, in 1972. Moving into her parents' new home brought her closer with the one person who was never fond of James and his smooth-talking ways: Todd's grandfather, Eugene Griffith. LL said his grandfather never liked his son-in-law because of the way he treated Ondrea. Little did Eugene know he was about to be caught in the crossfire.

VIOLENCE IN QUEENS

Eugene Griffith was a hardworking, mild mannered man of Caribbean descent who supported his family by working in the post office and as a custodian in the city school system. He also worked for New York City's voluntary auxiliary police force to help out in the community. LL credits Griffith with being his

Run-DMC's songs and style shaped hip-hop culture and brought it to mainstream media. They were pioneers in the hip-hop movement and influenced the next generation of rap artists. In this 1988 photograph, members of Run-DMC, Joseph "Run" Simmons *(left),* Darryl "DMC" McDaniels *(center),* and Jason "Jam Master Jay" Mizell *(right)* pose at the 31st Annual Grammy Awards.

role model and father figure during his troubled childhood. When Eugene wasn't working, he kept himself busy with jobs around the house, but "would stop and listen to [Todd] as if he were the only person in the world."

One of the biggest impressions Griffith left on his young grandson was a love for music. Eugene was a tenor saxophone player who loved jazz, often playing his favorite Billie Holiday or Duke Ellington records throughout the day. Sometimes he would play the music so loudly that his wife, Ellen, would yell at him to turn it down. Unlike the fights of Todd's parents, when his grandparents fought about things like loud music, the arguments were more "hilarious" than malicious, like "Alice and Ralph Kramden from *The Honeymooners*," LL has said.

Ellen Griffith stood a little more than five feet tall, but her influence on LL could not be measured. Ellen was strict and strong willed, and she asserted more authority than her small size would suggest. She was a devout Catholic, and she brought Todd to St. Bonaventure Church in Jamaica, Queens, every Saturday and Sunday, where he sang in the church choir. LL said his grandmother was "tough on the outside and tough on the inside," but "that she really knew how to take care of her family and be a caring mother." She even taught Todd his first rhyme: "If a task is once begun, never leave until it's done/Be the labor great or small, do it well or not at all."

Of all the things Ellen did for her family over the years, nothing was more important than the night she saved their lives. According to LL, his mother arrived home from her job at the Northport VA Medical Center at 1:00 A.M. on a hot August night to find her estranged husband waiting for her in his car with a 12-gauge shotgun sitting on his lap. When Ondrea reached the front door, James fired at her and then at Eugene, who had rushed to the door after the sound of the first shot jolted him from his chair. Todd had been sleeping but ran out of his room to see firsthand the damage his father had done.

Eugene and his daughter both lay wounded on the ground, Ondrea moaning in agony. After running outside to scold James as he sat in his car with his empty shotgun, Ellen called the police. When the ambulance didn't show up fast enough, LL's tiny grandmother managed to get her daughter and husband into the car and rush them to the hospital. Eugene had been shot in his stomach. The damage was so severe that the doctors had to remove parts of his intestines. Ondrea's bullet wound was in her lower back. The shotgun pellets had spread and hit her spine, leaving her unable to walk. Despite their extensive injuries, Ondrea and Eugene survived.

Todd's father fled the scene and moved to California, where he changed his name to Jimmy Nuña to avoid being caught. Ondrea eventually dropped the case and let her ex-husband off the hook without being prosecuted. This would not be the last time he would negatively impact his son's life, however.

RECOVERY AND ROSCOE

Although she survived the ordeal, Ondrea was hospitalized for six months. During her stay, she was under the care of an assistant physical therapist LL called Roscoe in his autobiography. It became Roscoe's mission to help Ondrea walk again. Within three months, she was out of her wheelchair. By the time she checked out of the hospital, she was walking on her own. LL said Ondrea felt Roscoe was largely responsible for

HEALING THROUGH MUSIC

Twenty-five years after his father shot his mother, LL Cool J wrote the song "Father" for his 1997 album *Phenomenon* to share the story of the shooting and his parents' separation:

She turned around heard the shotgun click.
My pops said, "you think that you could leave me?"
He blasted my moms in the back.
She fell down screamin', I can't forget that.
My grandfather tried to close the do'.
He got shot ten times in the stomach yo, for real.

her rehabilitation, and that may have contributed to her falling in love with him.

   After returning home from the hospital, Ondrea began dating Roscoe. She had just bought a small house for her and Todd in the North Babylon area of Long Island, and Roscoe stayed there all the time. LL recalled that, when Ondrea went to work each day, Roscoe drank and used drugs without bothering to hide his behavior. To make things worse, Roscoe viciously abused him. It didn't take long for Todd to realize Roscoe wasn't going to be any better as a father than his real dad. LL recalled,

> Roscoe would beat me for just about anything. He would beat me for watching television, for lookin' out the window, for lookin' at him funny. . . . He didn't need a good reason. It was just a power trip. . . . He would rotate beating me with extension cords, vacuum cleaner attachments, and fists. He would punch me in the chest and knock the wind out of me—and then tell me to "raise up," get up for another punch.

LL compared what it was like living with Roscoe to "sleeping in a cemetery with a dragon." The abuse was mental as well as physical. Roscoe harassed Todd constantly and forced him to do whatever he said. LL later described the beatings in the song "Father":

> This therapist got up in her head.
> Led her to believe without him she'd be dead.
> You know, they fell in love with one another.
> Everything seemed right that's word to mother.
> Until I started getting' beatings every day.
> Sometimes for going outside to play.
> Late at night on my knees I'd pray.
> A young child, wishin' the pain would go away …

On the weekends, Todd went back to Queens to visit his grandparents, where he got to play with his friends—and avoid Roscoe's beatings. He looked forward to the visits every week and was devastated if for some reason he couldn't go. LL described his life at that time as the "tale of two Todds." At his grandparents' house, he experienced "a close-knit family environment, where there was plenty of food, laughter, and love." When he returned home, he has said, he had to endure a man whose "sole purpose seemed to be to make [Todd's] life a living hell."

The abuse took place for four years without anybody, including Todd's mother, witnessing the truth. Ondrea didn't believe Todd's stories about Roscoe until she finally saw it for herself and "went bananas," jumping on his back and giving him a bloody lip. She eventually left Roscoe and moved back in with her parents, but the damage had been done. LL said the mental and physical pain somehow led to his now-famous habit of wearing hats all the time—almost as a security blanket. Until his starring role more than 20 years later in the 1995 movie *Out-of-Sync*, LL would never be seen publicly without one of his trademark caps.

The violence he learned at home followed him to school. LL was a bully and got into frequent fights. Later he attributed the inner rage he felt at that time to the abuse he had taken from Roscoe. He said that because he was defenseless at home, "on the streets [he] wasn't going to let anybody else beat [him]."

Todd was a Bruce Lee fan and would practice moves he learned from the martial arts legend's movies on his classmates. LL attributed more than fighting moves to his childhood idol: "The person that made me want to make movies, and the reason I do films, is Bruce Lee," LL told NY Rock Web site. "He was an incredible actor, and he had a lot of charisma . . . I loved Bruce Lee."

Todd had some real-life role models who prevented him from getting into real trouble—especially his gym teacher, Joel Asher, who "conducted himself like a man and showed [Todd]

As a child, LL Cool J had many influences. One of his idols was martial arts master and movie star, Bruce Lee. LL Cool J has said that after watching Bruce Lee in films, he too wanted to make movies. Photographed above is LL's childhood idol, Bruce Lee.

respect." Mr. Asher carried a plastic bat with him to keep the students in line, but everybody knew "behind that plastic bat was love." Todd also played Little League football for four years and kept busy with other activities like karate, wrestling, and gymnastics. Most of all, Todd spent his free time writing rhymes and rapping with his friends. Hip-hop was starting to take over the streets of New York—and Todd's life.

One day when Todd got home from school, his grandfather called him into the attic. He had bought the 11-year-old a present that would change the course of the young boy's life and hip-hop music forever. It wasn't the dirt bike Todd had been begging for and dreaming about for months. Instead, Eugene had bought a set of turntables, a mixer, two speakers, and a microphone. Todd now had everything he needed to become LL Cool J.

James Todd Smith Becomes LL Cool J

By 1979, the music scene was poised for change. For the last half of the 1970s, disco artists like Donna Summer and the Bee Gees had dominated the radio waves. Even rock and roll artists recorded disco records to cash in on the popularity of the genre, like the Rolling Stones song "Miss You" and the Beach Boys tune "Here Comes the Night." When Chic released "Good Times" in the summer of 1979, six of the top ten songs on the Billboard chart were disco songs. On August 18, when "Good Times" hit number one only three disco songs remained in the top ten. By September 22, disco had completely fallen out of the top ten. Disco was dead.

The irony was that even though "Good Times" was one of disco's final hit songs, its music helped propel hip-hop beyond

New York City and into the mainstream. When the Sugarhill Gang's band recreated Chic's music for "Rapper's Delight" in the autumn of 1979, radio programmers found a new genre of music to play instead of disco. Hip-hop was suddenly more than just an inner-city novelty. It was fresh. It was new. It was an inspiration to many would-be rappers, including Todd Smith, who realized his dream of being a hip-hop superstar could one day become a reality.

DETERMINED TO BE HEARD

It was a Sugarhill Gang concert that fueled Todd's passion for performing. Todd's mom took him to their concert at the Harlem Armory when he was 11 years old. The show came to an abrupt ending when somebody shot a gun into the air, but what Todd saw that night changed his life forever. "That concert gave me the yearning to go where I am now and to do what I'm doing today," LL said in his autobiography. "I could see myself up on stage with the mike in my hand, people screaming and rocking, and me just loving it."

LL said he went home after the show and worked on his rhymes in front of the mirror. Even though he didn't love his voice, he eventually found what types of rhymes sounded best coming from him instead of simply copying the style of other artists. Some rappers had a very limited vocabulary, but Todd's language skills allowed him to express himself in an original way. One of the rhymes he perfected in front of the mirror showed his talent for weaving challenging words into his lyrics: "When I commence with excellence, it eradicates levels of pestilence."

By the time Todd was 13 years old, "he was determined to be heard," and to make his mark on the hip-hop scene, so he did everything he could to make that happen. He spent hour after hour recording tapes in his basement, perfecting his raps. He knew that he needed to join forces with the biggest DJ in his neighborhood if he really wanted his big break.

Disco music gained popularity in the 1970s, dominating the music charts and defining the decade. In this 1978 photograph, club-goers dance to disco music in New York City's legendary Studio 54. By 1979, the decade and its soundtrack were coming to an end.

Jay Philpot was that DJ. Jay was a 5'11", 240-pound state heavyweight wrestling champion. He had the latest equipment and the loudest sound system in the neighborhood.

(continues on page 34)

THE SUGARHILL GANG

Nobody influenced LL Cool J—and many other would-be rappers—to start rhyming more than three MCs called the Sugarhill Gang. Their 1979 smash hit "Rapper's Delight" was the first song that bridged the gap between the hip-hop underground and the mass-market appeal of pop music. "It changed the face of music," LL said. ". . . to me they brought rap to a whole other level. They put rap on the map."

Unlike Kool DJ Herc, Afrika Bambaataa, Grandmaster Flash, and the other fathers of rap music who were more interested in making their audience dance and creating a new culture through music than they were in selling records across the country, the Sugarhill Gang accepted and embraced their crossover status. "They had no local expectations to fulfill, no street reputations to keep, no regular audience to please, and absolutely no consequences if they failed," said Jeff Chang.

Although Chang described Sugarhill Gang's "partly stolen rhymes" performed by "the very definition of a crew with no style" as somewhat of a "sham," the record's influence could not be denied. In the height of the disco era, this 15-minute epic borrowed music from Chic's disco classic "Good Times" and created a dance floor anthem that would eventually sell more than 2 million copies and crack the Billboard Top 40. Suddenly, hip-hop was to be taken seriously by radio programmers, club DJs, and record executives. It was a legitimate musical genre that would eventually redefine popular music. "For the rest of the world, beyond the Bronx and outside of New York, rap had arrived," hip-hop author and journalist S.H. Fernando Jr. said in the *The Vibe History of Hip Hop*. "And [more than] 20 years later, propelled by the vibrant and dynamic urban culture of hip-hop, it hasn't stopped moving and grooving yet."

The 1979 song "Rapper's Delight" by the Sugarhill Gang was one of the first hip-hop hit singles; a sign of the changing times. The Sugarhill Gang *(above* in 2001) was a direct influence on LL Cool J. After attending a Sugarhill Gang concert when he was 11 years old, the young Todd Smith knew what he wanted to do with his life.

(continued from page 31)

LL said that Jay "drew a crowd wherever he went" thanks to his undeniable skills and a bass that could be heard from blocks away. Todd wanted to "grab the mike and rock with his beat so bad [he] could taste it." He begged Jay all summer to let him rap. Jay remembered the 13-year-old Todd as a "hyperactive, had-too-much-sugar-in-the-morning-kid," but he eventually agreed to let Todd perform at a block party on 113th Avenue in Queens. Unfortunately, Jay's equipment wasn't working that day, so the anxious Todd searched out somewhere else to show off the rhymes he had been practicing for more than two years. Down the block, another DJ was mixing records and Todd approached him about rapping over his beats. He agreed and together they stepped into hip-hop history.

LL Cool J's first public performance took place in front of a block full of people who couldn't have known that they were witnessing the beginning of a hip-hop legacy. The young teenager's performance commanded attention with a routine he "rehearsed in [his] bedroom and in [his] head in school, when [he] should have been paying attention to Miss Beberman." The DJ mixed "Good Times" with "Dance to the Drummer's Beat" and LL said he "let it all roll out." According to him, "It just flowed." The most important person in the crowd was Jay Philpot, who was stunned by what he saw. LL said that Jay "couldn't believe that this little kid was rocking like that."

The block party was a sign of things to come. Jay was so impressed, he started picking up Todd from his grandmother's house and taking him to parties, where the two of them would perform. They weren't in it for the money—they didn't make a lot from their performances, and often they didn't even get paid. "We lived in the same neighborhood, and he was a guy that had talent and I took him under my wing," Philpot recalled in Stacy Guerasева's book *Def Jam, Inc.* Soon, the two of them

James Todd Smith became LL Cool J when he was 14 years old. Short for "Ladies Love Cool James," the name was derived after hours of deliberation and a talk with his friend, Playboy Mikey D. Now that he had his hip-hop name, all LL needed was a record contract.

were playing parties every other weekend and building a reputation. They also created entirely new names for themselves. Jay became Cut Creator. Todd's new name came about after a lot of deliberation.

INTRODUCING LADIES LOVE COOL JAMES

It was 1982 and Todd was 14 years old. He knew he needed a catchy hip-hop name like his idols Grandmaster Flash and the Sugarhill Gang, but his current name, J-Ski, wasn't quite right. "Around this time it seemed like every other rapper had a ski on the end of his name," LL said. "There was Luvbug Starski, Busy B-Starsky, Mike-ski, and a whole bunch of assorted Skis. I wanted to be different." Sitting on the floor of his mother's house in Long Island, something about the name Cool J, which stood for Cool James, stood out to him. "To me cool would never be played out," he said. "It seems like cool has been around since the beginning of time." After hours of thought, Todd officially became Cool J. The first person he told was his friend and rhyme-writing partner Playboy Mikey D. Playboy told him that he liked Cool J, but there was something missing from the name. He suggested Ladies Love Cool J. LL Cool J was born.

Now that he had a hip-hop name and a DJ, all LL wanted was a record contract. He visited record stores and wrote down the names of all the companies that produced rap records. LL sent his homemade demo tape to every hip-hop label he could find, including Sugar Hill Records, Tommy Boy Records, CBS, Island, Electra, and Profile. Within a few weeks, the rejection letters started showing up in the mail. "None of the record companies were feeling my art," LL recalled. "But something inside me told me to keep trying. And I persevered."

Ondrea Smith did all she could to keep her son's dream alive as well. She cashed her income tax refund check and bought LL the drum machine that allowed him to record his own beats and rap over them for the first time. Finally, LL could record a more professional-sounding demo tape, but where would he send it? Most of the record labels he'd tried had already turned him down. A relatively unknown New York University student named Rick Rubin was one of LL's last hopes. LL found Rubin's name on the back of a 12-inch record he had produced for T-La Rock and Jazzy J called "It's Yours." LL copied down Rubin's name and address and sent him a demo tape. Then he waited.

Putting Hip-Hop on the Map

Rick Rubin's NYU dorm room was the epicenter of hip-hop in the early to middle 1980s. Rubin was a guitar player in a punk band named Hose and a hip-hop DJ in his spare time. His love and keen ear for all types of music led him to start one of the most important and influential hip-hop labels of all time, Def Jam. Before Def Jam brought New York's inner-city music to the masses, rap was mostly an underground genre. With a few notable exceptions, such as the Sugarhill Gang's popular single "Rapper's Delight," hip-hop had barely made an impact on mainstream America and the Billboard charts. That was about to change.

Rubin was trying to talk his friend Russell Simmons into becoming a partner on the Def Jam label at the time LL was

Russell Simmons *(above)* collaborated with music producer Rick Rubin to start Def Jam Records. The label
that began in a New York University dorm room is now
a multimillion-dollar corporation synonymous with hip-hop
music. The first single released by Def Jam was LL Cool J's
"I Need a Beat," in 1984.

waiting to hear Rubin's feedback. Simmons had been involved in hip-hop for years with his Rush Productions imprint, which was one of the biggest labels in New York City at the time—largely thanks to Simmons's brother Run, who fronted Run-DMC. Rubin had four independent hip-hop hits already but needed Simmons's help with tours, artist management, and major labels. Simmons agreed and with $6,000, Def Jam was born. With their new label in place, they were ready to sign, record, and release records from some of the up-and-coming artists in the area, some of whom were already hanging out in Rubin's dorm room.

Three of Rubin's friends called themselves the Beastie Boys. The Beasties were three rowdy teenagers from Brooklyn, and they were the first white artists in hip-hop to have a measurable influence on the scene. Today, the Beastie Boys are one of the few acts from the early days of hip-hop who are still enjoying success more than 20 years later.

One of the three Beastie Boys, Adam Horovitz, a.k.a. Ad-Rock, lived relatively close to Rubin's dorm. He spent a lot of time there helping Rubin sort through the hundreds of demo tapes sent by aspiring rappers looking for their big break. Horovitz and Rubin were growing tired of listening to all the demos because, according to Rubin, most of them "were horrible."

One tape, though, immediately caught Horovitz's attention. In Def Jam, Inc., Horovitz recalled hearing LL Cool J's demo tape: "I can't say it was great . . . but it was different, and I liked it. There was something about it that just struck us as funny, and we wanted to hear it over and over again. I eventually learned that when something makes you laugh, that's a really good sign."

A MEETING OF THE MINDS

When LL got home from school that day and heard his grandmother speak the words "Some guy named Rick called," he knew right away this was a pivotal moment. "Suddenly it

Hip-hop trio the Beastie Boys were friends with Rick Rubin when he was attending NYU. One of the group's members, Adam Horovitz *(right)*, was hanging out in Rubin's dorm room and heard LL Cool J's demo. Horovitz knew the demo was unique and contributed to LL Cool J's signing to Def Jam.

seemed that all those months of writing, sending out tapes, getting rejection letters, writing, sending out more tapes, getting rejected again and again had paid off," LL recalled in his autobiography. "One telephone call made all the pain and torture and perseverance mean something. It was one of the happiest moments in what seemed to be a hard-luck life."

LL was the first person Rubin ever called based on the strength of his demo tape. They met for the first time in front of Rubin's NYU dorm, and LL recalled the first thing he said to the Jewish-American producer: "Yo! I thought you were black!" Until that moment, LL thought that hip-hop was a genre written, produced, and performed only by African Americans. It stunned him that two white Jewish guys had discovered him, but he didn't let his amazement faze him. "I didn't care if Rick Rubin was purple and worshipped penguins," LL said. "He could have been Ronald McDonald, as long as I got a record deal."

They went up to Rubin's tiny, crowded room and immediately Rubin played him some of the beats programmed in his drum machine. LL took to some of them and wrote lyrics on the spot. Within a day, they recorded their first song together, "I Need a Beat." Rubin knew it was something special and brought it to Simmons, who recognized that they had a hit on their hands. In November of 1984, "I Need a Beat" was the first record ever released on Def Jam. The song not only got the newly formed label off the ground but also showcased the 16-year-old's talents and intelligence, with rhymes full of challenging lyrics that nobody else in hip-hop was writing at the time:

> I syncopate it and design it well well
> Beat elevates-vates the scratch excels-cels
> All techniques are a combination
> of skills that I have, thought narration.

The single was out for less than a week when LL heard DJ Red Alert play it on the radio. Even though Red Alert talked over the song the whole time, LL considered it an honor to hear his song broadcasted by one of the most respected DJs in New York. The first time LL ever heard "I Need a Beat" played in its entirety was during KISS-FM's Friday Night Countdown. He was at an arcade in Queens with some of his friends playing games when the song came on. As soon as he heard it, LL walked outside so he could take in the experience all by himself. With his friends inside listening to his song,

LL said he was standing outside "in a daze." "It was like time had slowed down, the Earth was spinning half time, and it was just me and my record," he recalled. "I felt so good. I felt I had kissed God."

TAKING IT TO THE STREETS

From then on, Rubin and Simmons booked LL Cool J to perform live around the city. His first paid performance was at the Manhattan Center for Science and Mathematics, a public high school in Harlem, just blocks away from the Apollo Theater and the Harlem Armory, where LL had once been so inspired by watching the Sugarhill Gang perform. The school's cafeteria was transformed into a concert hall, and its tables were pushed together to create a stage. On the way to the event, Cut Creator's car broke down. He and LL walked the rest of the way and made it to the school just in time for the performance—despite Cut Creator's nervousness about leaving his car on the side of the road in Harlem. With Cut Creator manning the turntables, LL ran on stage and could feel the anticipation of the crowd. "They were so hyped. I couldn't believe it," he remembered. "It's one thing to rhyme for your peeps around the way, but it's another thing to see total strangers going bananas for you." After the show, they had to spend most of their earnings towing the car back to Queens, but they still considered the show a success and thought the "whole experience had been priceless."

To hone LL's skills as a performer, Simmons sent the young rapper on the Fresh Fest Tour in the summer of 1985, not to perform, but to learn from the tour's headliners Run-DMC, the Fat Boys, and Whoodini. At the time, Run-DMC was riding high at the crest of hip-hop success, and LL was seeking that same type of celebrity and stage presence. "He was a sponge," LL's former tour manager Tony Rome said in *Def Jam, Inc.* about LL. "He would just sit there and watch the

(continues on page 46)

RUN-DMC

No group symbolized and shaped 1980s hip-hop like rap super-group Run-DMC. Composed of Russell Simmons's little brother Joseph "Run" Simmons, Run's best friend Darryl "DMC" McDaniels, and the most influential DJ of the era Jason "Jam Master Jay" Mizell, the group from Hollis, Queens, elevated hip-hop to an unimaginable level of national prominence and sold more than 20 million albums worldwide. Run-DMC achieved all this while redefining hip-hop style with their gold rope chains, black fedora hats, and laceless Adidas shoes.

"[Run-DMC] came at a time when rap was not fully embraced by [even] the urban culture . . . People can't understand how important they were in pop music history," editor of *DJ Times* magazine, Jim Tremayne told CNN in 2002. "They were absolutely as revolutionary as Elvis."

In 1983, their first single, with "It's Like That" on one side and "Sucker MCs" on the other, took New York by storm. It "sounded like no other rap at the time," according to All Music's Stephen Thomas Erlewine. "It was spare, blunt, and skillful, with hard beats and powerful, literate, daring vocals, where Run and DMC's vocals overlapped, as they finished each other's lines. It was the first 'new school' hip-hop recording."

The record single-handedly changed the direction of hip-hop and the sound it had developed during its first decade. "It's the first really hard beat in rap, sounding aggressive before the words have a chance to announce it," music journalist Sasha Frere-Jones wrote in *The Vibe History of Hip Hop*. "As much empty space as music, it's abstract noise compared to the smiley funk retreads and synths on the radio."

After the success of their first single, Run-DMC went on to break new ground in rap music, set multiple records, and establish numerous firsts in popular music. They were the first rap act with a video on MTV. They were the first rappers with a number one *Billboard* R&B single, a top-ten album, a gold record, a platinum album, and a Grammy nomination. They also paved the way for other rappers by being the first to appear on TV shows such as *Saturday Night Live* and *American Bandstand*, and on the cover of prominent music publications like *Rolling Stone* magazine.

With Rick Rubin as their producer and Russell Simmons's Rush Productions managing them, their 1986 album *Raising Hell* climbed to number three on the Billboard album charts, selling more than 3 million albums and becoming the highest-selling rap LP in history. The biggest single on the album was a collaboration with Aerosmith on their song "Walk This Way." It became the first song to bridge the rap and rock genres and was also the first rap song to crack *Billboard*'s Top 10 singles chart.

The living-legacy of the group came to a tragic end when Jam Master Jay was murdered in his Queens studio in October of 2002. The hip-hop world went into mourning, and DJs worldwide paid tribute to the man that had inspired many of them to step behind their first set of turntables. Within a month of the murder, Run announced that Run-DMC would never perform again, because their sound "wouldn't be the same" with one-third of the band gone forever. "Nobody wants to see Run and DMC without Jay," he said. "Run-DMC is officially retired. I can't get on stage with a new DJ."

(continued from page 43)

show and study you like a book. Run onstage is very brag-
gadocio; LL just formulated his show from some of what he
saw. He didn't really steal anything, but he got ideas and he
just improved upon those ideas." To LL, Run-DMC were more
than role models, they were competitors. "From the start, LL
was clearly in competition with Run, who had always been
the youngest; the slim, cute guy. Whenever they got a chance,
LL and Run would battle-rap each other in the Rush office,"
Gueraseva said.

THE BIG SCREEN

After LL returned from the Fresh Fest Tour, Simmons introduced him to Cornell Clark, a highly respected music manager
at the time. Clark managed some of Simmons's other acts,
such as Kurtis Blow, who during that period was one of hip-
hop's biggest stars. Clark talked LL into hanging out on the set
of the movie Rick Rubin and Russell Simmons were making
called *Krush Groove.* Clark told LL, "Just go down there and let
them feel your presence. They will have to use you. They need
you." He was right.

   Krush Groove starred Rubin as a young record producer
trying to launch a record label from his dorm room. It featured many of the aspiring artists from Def Jam and Rush
productions, including Run-DMC, the Beastie Boys, the Fat
Boys, Kurtis Blow, and, thanks to Clark's advice, a cameo from
LL Cool J. The movie's story depicted Run-DMC's struggles
with fame and their dilemma over whether to stay signed to
their brother's struggling label or move to a major label in
search of fame and fortune. After hanging out on the set day
after day, LL finally got his break when Simmons and Rubin
talked the film's writers and directors into including a scene
where LL barged into Rubin's dorm room and demanded a
live audition. The scene lasted barely more than a minute, but
it was the first of many movie roles for LL, and it exposed him
to a much larger audience than he could have reached with

The still image above shows Buffy The Human Beat Box of the Fat Boys in the 1985 movie *Krush Groove,* which is based on the early days of Def Jam Records. Russell Simmons convinced the film's writers and directors to include LL Cool J in the film. LL made a scene-stealing cameo in his first big screen performance.

just a music video. The song he performed in *Krush Groove* was "I Can't Live Without My Radio," which appeared on his first full-length album, *Radio*.

SETBACKS BEFORE SUCCESS

Before his first album was finished, LL suffered a huge loss: the death of his grandfather. It was devastating for LL to lose the one positive father figure in his life, just before he really could have shared his success with him and made him proud. "It was the single most painful event in my life," LL said in his autobiography. "My grandfather was the only man in my life who had never disappointed me. And his death hurt me to the core." The loss led LL to withdraw from the rest of his family, including his grandmother, who refused to let him skip school because of his rap career. "She knew that no matter what happened in my music career, having a diploma was important," LL said. She gave LL a choice: Either focus on school or move out of her house. "I was thinking, if my grandfather were alive he'd understand. He wouldn't be on my back like this," LL said. So LL dropped out of school and moved out. With nowhere to go, he slept on subway trains for two weeks until Cornell Clark offered to let LL live in the basement of his place in Queens. Living in that basement, LL finished writing the lyrics to *Radio*. "Cornell saved me," LL said.

"LL'S GONE GOLD"

In September of 1985, Def Jam closed a $2 million deal with CBS, marking the first time a major label got involved in hip-hop. CBS was looking to update its urban music roster and become more relevant. "There was nothing streetwise or fresh, or reflective of more youthful urban hip-hop culture whatsoever at [CBS]," said Steve Ralbovsky, who worked in the A&R department of CBS's Columbia Records label, and who happened to be an old friend of Russell Simmons. When Ralbovsky's boss asked him about doing a deal with then power-house hip-hop label Tommy Boy Records, Ralbovsky turned him instead toward his friend Russell's fledgling Def Jam label. A few weeks later, the deal was done.

The deal worked out between CBS and Def Jam called for four records by four different artists to be released that year. The first album released as part of the deal was *Radio* in December of that year "and it became a hit with both consumers and critics," Guerasava wrote. "No one had ever heard anything like it." "*Radio* is a minimalist wonder of stark drum-machine beats, wikky-wikky scratch attacks, chain-saw guitar accents, and dazzlingly evocative rhymes," wrote *Spin* editor Sia Michel in *The Vibe History of Hip Hop*.

Rubin took full advantage of CBS's marketing budget to promote the album on the streets, in record stores, and with the press. The promotions and press events created a groundswell of support for LL's newest single "Rock the Bells," which immediately went gold. Michel counted it as "one of the greatest hip-hop singles of all time." Agreeing with the song's lyric: "it ain't rock and roll," Michel wrote it was "heavy metal, only funkier." In less than a year, "Rock the Bells" sold more than a million copies and went platinum. This single debuted at number five on *Billboard*'s top R&B singles chart, "which for a rap single was unheard of," LL recalled. "*Billboard* wasn't even charting rap back then."

In March of 1986, Columbia Records marketing director Jeff Jones interrupted Ralbovsky on a phone call in his office by placing a note on his desk. The note was a first for Def Jam. It said: "LL's gone gold." Ralbovsky hung up the phone so he could call the person who would be the most excited by the news. "Your grandson's record just went gold!," Ralbovsky told LL's grandmother Ellen Griffith. "Everyone from the artists to the staff at both Def Jam and CBS was thrilled," Gueraseva said. *Time* magazine called LL Cool J the country's hottest rap star. That spring, Simmons and Rubin visited Los Angeles and were stunned by LL's popularity on the West Coast. By that time, L.A. radio stations were playing almost every song recorded on *Radio*. LL was an instant national celebrity.

MONEY PROBLEMS

Unlike the days when LL would perform at neighborhood parties for little or no money, fortune accompanied the fame he received with the release of *Radio*. LL was amazed that he could earn such a great living from rapping. "I couldn't believe they were paying me so much money to do the thing I really loved doing, something I would do for free," he said. "I remember holding that first check for $50,000 and thinking I had hit the lottery." The only other job he had ever held was as a paperboy delivering the *New York Post*, making $2.50 per day and dealing with "rude and nasty" people at the crack of dawn. Having done a job he hated so much only made him appreciate his new life and the money that came with it all the more.

LL used his royalty checks to go on a spending spree. He bought his mom the car he had always promised her. He purchased gold chains for himself, and, "... plenty of Kangols.... My look had to be right. And it started with the hat," he said. "Mentally I wasn't right until I had on my hat ... and the more people that wondered and questioned me about why I wore hats, the more pleasure I got out of wearing them." Next he bought himself a convertible Mercedes and a red Audi 5000, which would later be pictured on the cover of his sophomore album *Bigger and Deffer*. He purchased fur coats for himself and his grandmother. He rented limos just to drive around the city and drink expensive champagne with his friends. His legendary overspending and overindulgence were famous, and he flaunted his wealth every chance he could, paving the way for present-day hip-hop's money-centric themes.

The cash and fame brought LL a whole new set of problems. Advisers, managers, and accountants suddenly appeared on the scene to give financial advice and to figure out how they could secretly take a cut for themselves. LL recalled:

> When you're an 18- or 19-year old kid hooked up to middle-aged, sophisticated businessmen who have been through myriad scenarios involving money, you don't have a chance…I saw crooked lawyers and crooked accountants early in my career . . . some of those accountants and business managers can plan some pretty devious ways to get to your money. The young up-and-coming star is defenseless.

THE BIG SPLIT

LL Cool J's celebrity and money still couldn't make him feel entirely secure. He wasn't sure he was getting what he deserved—either financially or in terms of attention and respect from Def Jam. Breakthrough artists like Public Enemy, the Beastie Boys, and Run-DMC were taking some of Rubin's and Simmons's focus away from him. "Somebody had to do the work for the other artists, and it was the same people who were doing the work for him," his former comanager and best friend Brian Latture said in *Def Jam, Inc.* "Anybody on Def Jam, he felt that he was responsible for their successes. Almost like he gave birth to the label and he's part of the reason why they're there." Gueraseva added, "With so many artists being managed by the same company, favoritism was inevitable." This rift between LL and Rubin changed LL's relationship with Def Jam and the sound of his music.

When it was time to get back in the studio and record a second album in late 1986, the strife between Rubin and his

In the early days of his career, LL Cool J was never seen without his signature Kangol hat. LL Cool J made his first appearance without his trademark hat in the movie *Out of Sync* in 1995.

one-time prodigy had reached critical mass. Rubin was busy making another movie with Run-DMC named *Tougher Than Leather*, and he wasn't interested in continuing his and LL's winning formula together. "Their relationship had experienced such a dive over the past several months that LL, who was originally supposed to be in the film, was taken off the project," Gueraseva said. She went on to say that Rubin thought their "pure, naïve energy" would never be repeated.

LL needed a new producer and Russell Simmons introduced him to Dwayne Simon and Darryl Pierce, who were given the name L.A. Posse by Jam Master Jay. They were an inexperienced two-man production team from Los Angeles that Russell was trying fit somewhere into the Def Jam mix. Working on LL's new album provided a perfect opportunity for them to make their first mark on the industry.

MAKING *BIGGER AND DEFFER*

LL's initial meeting with Simon and Pierce in the Chinatown studio where *Radio* was recorded was "very uncomfortable" according to Simon. "This guy's a star. We're nothing," he thought on first meeting the platinum-selling rapper. After the meeting, Simon and Pierce tried to follow LL out of the studio to see what kind of car he drove, but they lost him. When they arrived at the subway station, they saw LL standing on the other side of the platform. They were shocked to find out that he still rode the train to the studio instead of driving one of his fancy cars. From then on, their relationship during the recording process was never uncomfortable again.

While they became acquainted with each other, LL expressed his anger toward Rick Rubin and Def Jam. Simon said that "all [LL] wanted was a little respect." He also wanted the meteoric success and support that Run-DMC was receiving. To take a stand and set LL Cool J apart, he and Simon agreed that LL would never wear Run-DMC's trademark Adidas clothing anymore and would only wear Nike.

Within a couple weeks, they recorded four songs but kept working until they had written 16 tracks, including a ballad. Simon told LL that the ballads on *Radio* were "the bomb" and persuaded him to write and record a slow love song named "I Need Love." Russell Simmons hated the ballad when Simon played it for him. He played it for Rubin, who also thought it was terrible and was looking instead for something similar to what LL had recorded on *Radio*. "But this was a sophomore album," Simon recalled. "You have to grow, you don't stay in the ninth grade forever. Nobody dug that record, except the people that made it." The people who made it—LL Cool J and the L.A. Posse—turned out to have the measure of what America wanted to hear next from LL Cool J.

SINGLES AND VIDEOS

In March 1987, the first single from *Bigger and Deffer*, "I'm Bad," hit the streets two months before the album's June release date. It was an immediate hit. The next week, "I Need Love" hit the radio waves before Def Jam could even release it as a single. Rick Rubin was still completely uninvolved in the album—including uncharacteristically not having a say in the cover art. LL loved the cover picture of him, dressed all in black leather with a red Kangol hat and Nike sneakers, standing on top of his Audi. When *Bigger and Deffer* was recorded and released, Rubin was in Los Angeles working on a soundtrack for the movie *Less Than Zero*. One of the soundtrack's songs, "Going Back to Cali," was the only collaboration between Rubin and LL since recording *Radio*. It was also the last song they ever worked on together.

When *Bigger and Deffer* hit store shelves in June, it was already a big success thanks to "I'm Bad" and "I Need Love." Critics and fans loved the album. The *Los Angeles Times* music critic went so far as to give him the edge over his mega-famous label mates: "In peak form, LL Cool J can rap faster than the speed of three Beastie Boys and deliver the kind of fresh imagery that runs circles around Run-DMC." Reviewer Connie Johnson went on to say that "LL is still his own greatest competition in the rap arena. Even when he doesn't top himself, he's still more original than most of his 'bust this!' contemporaries." Sia Michel said that although *Bigger and Deffer* is a concept album and the concept is LL's ego . . . at least LL had an album worthy of the self-proclaimed 'baddest rapper in the history of rap itself.'" Riding the wave of critical appreciation and unprecedented radio play, the album eventually went double platinum.

Two days after the album was released, LL left to headline the monumental coast-to-coast Def Jam Tour with Public Enemy, Whoodini, Stetasonic, Eric B. & Rakim, and Doug E. Fresh. It was one of the biggest hip-hop tours in history and ran at the same time as the American leg of the Run-DMC and Beastie Boys tour—giving Def Jam and Rush Productions a virtual monopoly on hip-hop concerts during the summer of 1987.

The Def Jam Tour became legendary not only for the music of virtually every act on the tour, many of whom would go on to become hip-hop legends, but also for the craziness that surrounded it. According to Stetasonic DJ Prince Paul, "At times, it was like a big frat party." When it came time to perform, LL brought along a huge stage set that Guerasava described as "a giant radio, two turntables, and a kind of rap castlelike structure." When the two tours combined to play one massive show in Atlanta, Georgia, LL couldn't set up the stage the way he wanted to and developed a bad case of stage fright. His tour manager, Tony Rome, calmed LL's nerves by telling him, "You gotta go back to what you first did, go out there and act like you don't have nothing, and you [are] just trying to get on." The show went on to be one of LL's best performances on the tour.

LL was making a name for himself on MTV as well. He didn't make any videos for *Radio*, so he was anxious to show his personality and style to his fans. His first video was for "I'm Bad" and featured LL in his signature outfit, just as the police APB at the beginning of the song described it: "*Wearing a black Kangol, sweatsuit, gold chain, and sneakers.*" In the song, LL shows his self-promotional skills, while retaining some of the comedic elements that got his demo tape noticed in the first place: "I'm the pinnacle that means I reign supreme/And I'm notorious I'll crush you like a jelly bean/I'm bad."

The next video he made was for "I Need Love." Sia Michel said that in the video "poor little Todd sits all lonely and vulnerable in his humble white stretch limo." He looked far less lonely and vulnerable in his next video, the black-and-white classic for "Going Back to Cali" that showed him looking stylish and driving down a California street. Unfortunately for LL and Def Jam, one of the girls in the video was a minor and MTV refused to show the video until they imposed a black box over her. Once that issue was resolved, all three videos were shown continually in MTV's rotation, showcasing LL as the new face of hip-hop to a nationwide audience.

NEEDING AND FINDING LOVE

By late summer, "I Need Love" was on its way to becoming the first hip-hop song to reach number one on the Billboard R&B singles chart. LL said the song "put [him] in a whole other category as far as rappers were concerned. It was the first rap ballad to be a hit, and it was different from the bravado and hard, rough style many rappers had adopted . . . that was a real risk for me then. I could have come off as soft." Sia Michel said LL became "hip-hop's biggest sex symbol" and was "perhaps the only MC besides Tupac to be as loved by the ladies as he claimed to be." The song was a very personal one for LL, who said he wrote it during a time that he felt

LL Cool J is photographed with his wife, Simone, in 1999. When LL first met Simone, he was in the early stages of his rap career, enjoying the perks of his newfound fame. Simone was unlike the other star-struck women he met, because she was unfazed by his celebrity. The two began an on-and-off again relationship, and within two years of their first meeting, Simone gave birth to their first child, Najee Laurent Todd Eugene Smith.

he "really did need love" and was "feeling a lot of emptiness" in his life. "[I Need Love] came from the heart," LL recalled. "I had already made the circuit of groupies and was getting a little out of control. I felt like the ladies only wanted to be with LL Cool J. Nobody was feeling Todd. I wasn't sure if I even was." The song's first verse echoed the way he was feeling:

> When I'm alone in my room sometimes I stare at the wall
> And in the back of my mind I hear my conscience call
> Telling me I need a girl who's as sweet as a dove
> For the first time in my life, I see I need love.

By the time the song reached the top of the charts, LL realized he had found the love he claimed he needed so badly. Her name was Simone, and, after meeting her on Easter Sunday earlier in the year at her aunt's house, LL began dating her. Simone was "this tiny girl, wearing a lemon-colored sweater set with a long skirt . . . and alligator pumps" the day they met. She stood out to LL because he said she was one of the first women that, instead of treating him like a star, treated him like "So what?"

They hit it off, and their on-again off-again relationship began. At the time, LL wasn't willing to settle down with any woman, but Simone was special. There was something about her that made her stand out above all the other women in LL's life. Within two years, Simone gave birth to their first child and only son, Najee Laurent Todd Eugene Smith.

LL was at the hospital when Najee, which means "success" in Arabic, was born. LL Cool J was 21 years old, and he said he didn't know who he was at the time, let alone how to be a father. When Najee came home for the first time, LL realized all the work he would have to put into raising him, and he thought, "My youth and my freedom . . . are gone." Afraid of the responsibilities now facing him, LL fled. "All I wanted to do was drive around in my convertible Mercedes with my gold chains and with a girl in the passenger seat," LL recalled. "I wanted to be free. I didn't want to feel like I was handcuffed." So drive around in his convertible Mercedes he did, choosing a lifestyle of excess instead of a life with Simone and their newborn son.

Don't Call It a Comeback

Even after finding Simone, releasing consecutive hit albums, and experiencing nationwide fame, LL's career and personal life were about to take a turn for the worse. Although it appeared that LL Cool J had easily acquired everything a young man could want, he would soon find it a challenge to reestablish a relationship with a familiar troublemaker from his past—his father, who now called himself Jimmy Nuña.

LL was a 20-year-old millionaire, but those close to him worried that, even with all his money, his spending was out of control. "I had back-to-back platinum albums, was working on a third, and I had a million dollars in the bank," LL said. "And I had a $15,000 ring that spelled out my name across four fingers in diamonds." His weakness was cars. "I bought cars like most people buy shoes," he said. "I had one to fit every occasion." On a tour stop in Maryland during the Def Jam Tour, he bought a BMW on a whim and drove it back to New York. After the tour, he bought a white convertible Mercedes in Los Angeles for more than $100,000. He said his collection of luxury cars was up to 12, each of which was equipped with state-of-the-art electronics. He claimed it was nothing for him to spend $10,000 to $12,000 on a car stereo system. He even bought another car for his mom and for his comanager, Brian Latture.

Ondrea tried to keep track of her son's career and spending but knew she couldn't do it on her own. As a last resort, she turned to her ex-husband for help, despite his near-fatal attack on her 16 years earlier. Jimmy Nuña was brought in to manage his son's career because of his alleged business acumen. LL was willing to overlook Nuña's violent history and give him another chance to be a father figure and positive influence. "It doesn't matter how rotten or how much of a lowlife a child's father is, a kid wants to point to a man and say, 'That's my daddy,'" LL said in his autobiography.

Nuña's antics immediately became a problem for LL and everybody around him—especially those at Def Jam, who couldn't convince LL that his father was bad for him. "He wanted his father, so you couldn't tell LL anything," said Def Jam's then A&R director and business manager Faith Newman. "He had to figure it out on his own." Nuña had a huge influence on his son at the time, and LL refused to listen to anybody else. "LL stopped trusting us and having confidence in us," Lyor Cohen said. "He completely submitted to his father during that period … It was all about pushing that button of LL's, that insecure button."

BACKLASH

Faced with the pressure of making a third blockbuster album, LL got back into the studio to record *Walking with a Panther*. Because of contractual issues, only Darryl Pierce from L.A.

Posse was available to produce the album, meaning LL had only half of the team that had helped make *Bigger and Deffer* such a hit. After some time working together, the album was going nowhere. Russell Simmons brought in Public Enemy's producer Hank Shocklee, but even his considerable skills weren't enough to give LL what he needed the most. "You don't have that big song," Simmons told LL. "You need that big song!" On a flight from Los Angeles to New York,

PUBLIC ENEMY NO. 1

Chuck D, Flavor Flav, Terminator X, and the S1Ws composed the revolutionary rap group appropriately named Public Enemy. They not only redefined rap music but also single handedly reshaped hip-hop culture in the late 1980s and early 1990s. Straying away from the high-rolling lifestyle LL Cool J symbolized, which was full of gold chains, champagne, and groupies, Public Enemy rapped about the issues facing inner-city African-American youths. Their message unified the culture around a political message and a cause more important than cars and bank accounts.

"No act in the history of hip-hop felt more important than Public Enemy," *The Vibe History of Hip Hop*'s editor Alan Light wrote. "More than anyone else, they forced the world to take hip-hop seriously."

Their album *It Takes a Nation of Millions to Hold Us Back* was released in 1988 and was one of the most critically acclaimed LPs of the 1980s. *Spin* named it the second best album in the magazine's history, and VH1 recognized it as the twentieth greatest album of all time. Jeff Chang said that on it, Public Enemy "positioned themselves as heirs to James Brown's

LL wrote that song. By the time the plane landed, LL had completed the lyrics for "I'm That Type of Guy." He recorded the song that same night at the only open studio he could find. It would eventually become the Top 10 single Simmons was looking for, but its lyrics about stealing other men's girl-friends showed that LL was still wrapped up in bragging and boasting when the rest of the hip-hop community was ready for a change.

loud, black and proud tradition." He said that "within a month, the album had already sold a million copies and perhaps set off an equal number of debates."

Their next release didn't pull any punches either. *Fear of a Black Planet*'s rabblerousing anthem "Fight the Power" was a number one hit featured in Spike Lee's movie *Do the Right Thing* and served as a rallying cry for the African-American community. Flavor Flav's track "911 Is a Joke" called out emergency services for responding slowly to calls from African-American neighbor-hoods. " 'Fight the Power' and '911 Is a Joke' flew right in the face of government and racism," LL said in his book. "That whole movement talked about the black man educating himself and uplifting himself—both messages I was with totally."

To this day, Public Enemy remains in the spotlight. Their 2005 song "Hell No We Ain't All Right!" criticized George W. Bush and his response to Hurricane Katrina. At the same time, the self-proclaimed greatest hype man of all time, Flavor Flav, has starred in a series of VH1 reality shows, most notably his own series, the "Flavor of Love."

A NEW ERA IN RAP

Public Enemy ushered in a new era of rap music, as Run-DMC and LL Cool J had done in the early 1980s. Public Enemy's politically charged message gave the hip-hop community something to think about and listen to besides ego-driven lyrics and material possessions—exactly the things LL represented. In its review of *Walking with a Panther*, *Rolling Stone* claimed that "LL Cool J probably couldn't have picked a worse time to release [the album]." The backlash to LL and his new album was intense. "I had become the anti-Christ of rap," he recalled. "I was selfish, I was egocentric. People felt like I was not being honorable and I didn't represent where the black community should be heading."

The worst of the backlash showed up while he performed live. When LL appeared at a rally in Harlem, "the crowd broke into resounding boos when [he] took the stage, treating him like a diamond-dipped throwback to a shallower time," Sia Michel recounted in *The Vibe History of Hip Hop*. When he headlined the Nitro Tour to support *Walking with a Panther*, the crowds did not have a more favorable response to him. Among the acts supporting him were Slick Rick, N.W.A., and Too Short, all artists highly respected in urban America. When the tour kicked off, LL was no longer in the same esteemed category as his opening acts, having lost virtually all his street credibility in the hip-hop community. "By the time the tour hit the road, some of LL Cool J's hardcore fans had abandoned him, thinking he had become too 'soft,'" Stacy Gueraseva said. "At one outdoor concert, fans even threw objects at him."

To make things worse, Jimmy Nuña came along on the tour to wreak havoc every step of the way. "My pops . . . was constantly burning bridges and getting into beefs with people wherever we went," LL remembered. "Conflict was his middle name." From provoking fistfights with LL to getting arrested for brawling in a Miami hotel lobby, Nuña's troublemaking plagued the tour. "Nuña was extraordinarily mean-spirited,

Rap group Public Enemy changed the face of rap music with their socially aware lyrics, focus on political issues, media criticism, and African-American activism. The group raised the bar in the hip-hop world, making acts like LL Cool J seem frivolous and irrelevant. In the photograph above, Public Enemy's Chuck D *(left)* and Flavor Flav *(right)* perform in 1992.

calculated, disrespectful, and not particularity bright or savvy," recalled Lyor Cohen.

THE COMEBACK

LL knew he had to change his priorities if he wanted to win back his fans. Looking at his picture on the cover of *Walking with a Panther*, LL recognized that he represented everything wrong with hip-hop music. He admitted in an October 14, 1990, *Los Angeles Times* article that he "went off the deep end with the champagne and girls . . . thinking people liked to see me [that way]. But that's not right. They like my music. What does that [photo] have to do with rap and the streets? That wasn't me." The criticism was wearing on him, so he returned

LET THE BATTLE BEGIN

It wasn't only the critics and fans that turned against LL; other rappers also jumped on the anti-LL bandwagon, mocking him in their songs, album covers, and music videos. Feuds with rappers such as Ice-T and Wyclef Jean of the Fugees have plagued LL throughout his career. Kool Moe Dee started the most notable verbal war. Kool was one-third of an old-school hip-hop act from Brooklyn known as the Treacherous Three. After turning solo, one of his favorite things to rap about—and against—was LL Cool J.

An August 22, 1989, *USA Today* article said the feud between the two stars "represents the growing division between rappers like LL Cool J, who are crossing over into a huge pop audience, and purists like Kool Moe Dee, concerned about social issues confronting rap's traditional fans." Kool Moe Dee went on national television and told talk show host Arsenio Hall that LL was a bad role model. LL claimed he didn't want to be a role model. "I don't think the weight of the world should be on a person just because they do rap music," LL told *USA Today*. "I'm not asking someone to look up to me. I'm asking them to accept music for what it is."

Sporting his trademark dark wraparound sunglasses, Kool Moe Dee threw the first punch on vinyl with his second album, *How Ya Like Me Now.* The cover of the album showed a white jeep running over a red Kangol hat, and the title track attacked LL with lines like:

to his grandmother's basement to take stock of himself and the direction of his career. When she asked him what was wrong, LL told her that he didn't think he had it anymore. "I feel like all these other guys are getting over," he said. "It's changed so

It irked my nerve when I heard
A sucker rapper that I know I'll serve
Run around town sayin' he is the best
Is that a test?

LL proved he wasn't going to take the criticism without a fight. He fired back on his ferocious comeback song "Jack the Ripper," calling Kool Moe Dee a "washed up rapper."
Next, it was Kool's turn on the song "Let's Go:"

I'm formidable, unforgettable
You're submittable, you look pitiful
Yeah you're headstrong, but you're dead wrong
Wanna survive? Stick with the love songs
Take off your shirt, flex and flirt
And leave the real hard rhymes to the hard rhyme experts.

The battle continued to go back and forth with no clear winner—other than increased record sales and heightened notoriety for both rappers. The conflict set a precedent by showing rappers that a good way to make a name for themselves was to talk about other rappers in their rhymes. The trend even continued in the late 1990s, when a relatively unknown rapper named Canibus took a shot at LL. He wasn't fazed; after all, he'd been through it before.

much. I can't do it the way they do it. What's selling now is something totally different." Her six-word response helped her grandson turn his career around. She replied, "Oh baby, just knock them out." LL took the advice to heart and began writing songs for his fourth album, appropriately named *Mama Said Knock You Out*.

Russell Simmons and LL recruited legendary hip-hop producer Marley Marl to make the music for the entire album. The result was what AOL Music called "the hardest record [LL] ever made." Sia Michel said the sell-out controversy surrounding LL's previous album "resulted in LL's most convincing persona yet . . . It's not *what* he says that matters this time, it's *how* he says it." She called the album's title track "perhaps the hungriest song in hip-hop history." That song opens with the lines "Don't call it a comeback. I've been here for years." However, to music critics and the fans who questioned LL's integrity and intentions, the album did indeed signify a comeback, a return to the passion of his roots in hip-hop.

Awarding it five out of five stars, All Music Guide's Steve Huey claimed that on *Mama Said Knock You Out* "LL is at his most lyrically acrobatic, and the testosterone-fueled anthems are delivered with a force not often heard since his debut." "[The album] succeeded mightily," he said "making him an across-the-board superstar and cementing his status as a rap icon beyond any doubt."

Mama Said Knock You Out went on to be LL's fourth platinum LP and his top-selling album of all time. It spawned three hit singles—its title track, "The Boomin' System," and "Around the Way Girl"— and one of the most iconic hip-hop videos of all time. LL still wasn't willing to call it a comeback. "It's flattering for people to say comeback and veteran and pioneer," he told a *Los Angeles Times* reporter in an article published October 4, 1990. "I don't want those trophies, the longevity and comeback trophies. I just want people to know I've been here for years and continue to make my music." He may not

With the release of the album *Mama Said Knock You Out*, LL Cool J reestablished his hip-hop image and credibility. The album spawned three hit singles, and it is his top-selling album of all time. In 1991, he was awarded the MTV Video Music Award for Best Rap Video *(above)*.

have wanted certain accolades, but he did garner two awards for the album's title track. The first honor was the MTV Video Music Award for Best Rap Video, which LL Cool J won for the now-classic black-and-white video featuring a hooded LL ferociously rapping and shadowboxing in the middle of a boxing ring. The next honor he took home was on February 25, 1992, when he was given a Grammy Award for Best Rap Solo Performance—in only the second year that category was made a part of the Grammy Awards. "I remember sitting in the audience of Madison Square Garden . . . waiting for them to call my name," he recalled in his autobiography. "And they did. That moment was one of the sweetest. It was like everyone who ever said I couldn't do something was proved wrong that day."

A TURN FOR THE WORSE

With yet another platinum album under his belt, LL was at the peak of his career. Not only was he on the top of the rap world but also his musical resurgence led to other artistic opportunities. In 1992, LL appeared in his first significant movie role as Captain Patrick Zevo in the Robin Williams movie *Toys*. LL also turned in a groundbreaking performance as the first rap artist to appear on MTV's *Unplugged* series, and he performed at Bill Clinton's presidential inauguration in 1993. "Everything seemed perfect," LL recalled. "But I couldn't have been more wrong. Everything was definitely *not* perfect."

Although LL had many of the career highlights of which he'd always dreamed, his on-and-off relationship with Simone was far from ideal. Simone and LL were continually drawn together, although neither stopped dating other people to make their relationship exclusive. Simone gave birth to their first daughter, Italia, that year, but LL was still not faithful to the mother of his children. Not only that, Simone and the two children were living in a small two-bedroom condo, while their father was enjoying the luxuries of being a multimillionaire. "Simone, to her credit, never gave up on me," LL said. "She had

At the height of his career, LL Cool J was producing platinum albums, acting in movies, and even performing at presidential inaugurations. In the photograph above, he performs in front of the Lincoln Memorial as part of the 1993 presidential inauguration of Bill Clinton.

moved on with her life . . . but the bond between us was too strong for her to let me fail."

LL's acting career was getting off to a rough start as well. He was finally offered his first starring film role in 1995's *Out-of-Sync*. In the movie, he portrayed a DJ who had to choose between his music and his life on the streets. LL hoped the movie would launch his career as a leading man, but it bombed at the box office, only selling $9,000 in tickets. "The only thing memorable about it is that they talked him into removing his hat," his comanager Brian Latture said in *Def Jam, Inc.* "It was the first public image of LL without his hat." Hollywood veteran Debbie Allen directed the movie. LL felt that Allen, who was famous for her roles in movies like *Fame*, had done all she could do with the budget she had been given, but he recognized that his acting was terrible. "I should have paid them for the movie," he admitted.

Finally, LL also came to the conclusion that his father was not looking out for his best interests. "He wasn't taking care of my business properly," LL said. "He wasn't making sure my taxes got paid. He was ringing up personal stuff on corporate credit cards. And he wasn't looking out for my money as others around were stealing from me." As a result, LL was in debt to the IRS for more than $2 million and almost lost his house. He also felt that his father wasn't finding the best movie deals he could, and often he would not even pass along scripts for LL to review. His father's mismanagement forced LL to reevaluate the way he was going to manage his career in the future. "Today, I'm aware of every role, every offer, every deal, and every dime that comes through my camp" he said. "I'm involved with every decision."

Misplacing his trust in his father led LL to doubt whether he could even depend on his best friend and comanager Brian Latture. For starters, LL felt that Latture was spending too much time managing the rapper Nas. To compound matters, Latture neglected to follow LL's instructions to give money to Cornell Clark. Clark was dying of AIDS, and LL asked Latture to give him money to ease his pain. Latture didn't, and LL was devastated to find out the truth after his friend's death. "I had been badly burned," he said. "My best friend—my son's godfather and my manager—had betrayed me . . . There are no words to describe how disgusted I was and still am."

The pain in his personal life gave LL inspiration for the follow-up to *Mama Said Knock You Out.* "At the time I was feeling like I had nothing," he said in his autobiography. "No kids, no wife, no friends, no home, no career, no nothing." In his book, LL talked about the time he stood in the shower with tears pouring down his face: "I was crying for a woman I had treated like a dog, crying for the children I had abandoned, crying for my life, which I was just throwing away. And crying because I felt like I had been betrayed on every level. I had a broken heart." The new album was titled *14 Shots to the Dome,* and LL said that because his "spirit was disturbed throughout the recording and mixing," it "was the deepest thing [he] had ever done." That depth did not lead to a successful album, however, despite the huge marketing push Def Jam put behind it. According to *Rolling Stone* magazine's Al Weisel, *14 Shots to the Dome* "shot 14 blanks."

With all the disappointments piling up, LL said in his autobiography he got "the courage to clean house, something he needed to do for years." He parted ways with Brian Latture. Then LL went to the bank and froze the rest of his money so his father couldn't take any of it, and he severed ties with him as well. He enrolled in a class to get his GED and finish high school. "Going back to school got me back on track," he said. The final thing he needed to turn things around was a new manager. He turned to "one of the only people who was giving more than he was taking," his longtime spiritual adviser Charles Fisher. The two had met in 1995 when Fisher worked for Russell Simmons and ran LL's fan club. "[Charles] had been there at the very beginning of my career," LL recalled in his autobiography. "Over the years he kept popping up here and there ... with spiritual and cultural literature that he wanted [me] to read." Charles turned LL on to "everything from the Bible to the Koran," and LL said he "was drinking it up like [I] had been on the Sahara for ten years without a drop [of water]."

In 1992, LL Cool J founded Camp Cool J, a summer camp for inner-city kids. It was during this time that LL came to a turning point in his life. He realized the importance of family, children, and giving back to the community. In the photograph above, LL Cool J rides a float in the Macy's Thanksgiving Day Parade with some of the boys from his camp.

Thanks to Charles's guidance, LL said he made the decision to change his life for the better. When it came time to find a new person to help manage his career, LL thought Charles, who had discovered R&B singer R Kelly, was the perfect man for the job.

On his new righteous path, LL was ready to take on anything that came his way. More important, he was able to put everything into perspective and realize what is truly important to him, like children—his own and others. He founded Camp Cool J, a summer camp for inner-city youth that takes them away from difficult situations and places them in an environment that stresses cultural awareness through education and athletics. Perhaps this new outlook on life and endeavors such as Camp Cool J paved the way for his next big break.

A Decade of Love and Growth

After cleaning up his act, LL turned his life around in 1995. As luck would have it, one of his biggest flops would lead to one of his biggest opportunities and a major turning point in his life. Entertainment mogul Quincy Jones contacted LL and asked him to star in an NBC situation comedy called *In the House*, on which he would work with *Out-of-Sync* director Debbie Allen once again. Quincy Jones, whose daughter Kidada had once dated LL, wanted LL for the role of a former Oakland Raiders football player named Marion Hill. The premise of the TV show was that Hill needed money so badly that he rented out some of the rooms in his house. Debbie Allen played the woman who, along with her family, lived in Marion Hill's house. LL loved the role because of Marion Hill's

The cast of the television show *In The House, (left to right)* LL Cool J, Kim Wayans, Alfonso Ribeiro, and Maia Campbell, pose for this 1997 publicity photograph. With the sitcom, LL was expanding his career beyond music, as well as providing a positive image of African-Americans in the media.

clean lifestyle. "What really convinced me to do the show was that the character had a holistic approach to life—no drinking, no wild women, no drugs," LL said. "Just the way my life had become." In fact, one of the running jokes during the show's five-season run involved the other characters making fun of the alternative methods that Marion Hill used to heal his injuries, such as meditation and aromatherapy.

In the House came at time when things were looking bleak for him, LL said. The show gave him something positive to focus on and helped develop his acting skills. He said it also showed him what it was like to have a day job that required him, among other things, to do what he hated the most—wake up early. "[The show] gave me discipline," he said. "I had to get up early every morning—and anyone who knows me knows that is a real struggle." Most important, LL Cool J's work on *In the House* showed the world that he could move beyond music to become a TV star. He said in a February 10, 1996, *Los Angeles Times* article that he expected those involved in the hip-hop culture to embrace this decidedly mainstream move and say "Oh, LL's hustling, he's expanding, he's moving on even more, and that's good."

He continued to expand and move on with his next album, the double platinum *Mr. Smith*. The album spawned three top-ten singles, including the classic "Doin' It," and "Hey Lover," a song that saw him team up with R&B group Boyz II Men to make one of the biggest hits of his career. The song went all the way to number three on the Billboard charts and earned him his second Grammy Award for Best Rap Solo Performance. *Rolling Stone* writer Cheo H. Coker said the album's finer points proved LL was still talented enough that he need not rely on being such a ladies' man to be successful: "Maybe one day LL will realize that it's his electrifying flow, not his Casanova aspirations, that have made him a rap superstar for ten years running." LL agreed and finally decided to put his Casanova aspirations behind him once and for all.

A NEW CHAPTER

Simone was eight months pregnant with their second daughter and third child, Samaria, and LL was determined not to "bring another child into this world out of wedlock," so he proposed to Simone. She said yes and in August of 1995, LL

LL Cool J attends the 2003 premiere of the movie *S.W.A.T.* with Simone, Samaria, and Italia. After an eight-year relationship, LL married his longtime love, who was pregnant with their third child. The couple also has a son named Najee and a daughter, Nina Simone.

and Simone got married, legally binding the eight-year relationship that had already brought them two children, with a third just weeks away. Their fourth child, Nina Simone, was born in 2000. Simone wanted to postpone the wedding until after Samaria's birth, but LL refused to wait. "I didn't care about anything else once I made that decision," LL recalled. "There were already too many wasted moments in our life, and I wasn't about to waste any more." They had what LL called a "down-home wedding" in the backyard of their Long Island house. Only family and close friends attended, and everybody had to bring a potluck dish. Najee was the ring bearer, and Italia was the flower girl.

With calm and order restored to his personal life, LL could dive once again into broadening his artistic endeavors. In 1998, he released a tell-all autobiography titled *I Make My Own Rules* and an album to accompany the life stories in it, called *Phenomenon*. It was the first time LL told the world about the abuse he had endured growing up and the up-and-down nature of his life and career. The album *Phenomenon* gained notoriety for the public feud it sparked between LL and upstart rapper Canibus.

The fight started because of the lyrics of a song: One of the songs on *Phenomenon* featured other Def Jam rappers, including Method Man, Redman, DMX, and Canibus. One of Canibus's lyrics, referring to the crown-topped microphone tattoo on LL's right arm, addressed LL directly: "Yo L, is that a mic on your arm? Lemme borrow that." LL took the verse as an insult and responded with a blistering verse kicked off by these lines: "The symbol on my arm is off limits to challengers. You hold the rusty swords I swing the Excalibur." Canibus's verse was cut from the final song, but LL's response remained. When the original version of the song was leaked to the public, the fighting began all over again. After a few years of lyrically battling with LL, Canibus told VH1 that he decided the feud was a bad idea and sent the wrong message.

In the end, he said he wished he had never been asked to contribute a verse in the first place. "I do regret ever getting the phone call for '4,3,2,1' in the very beginning," he told VH1. "That's what started it all."

BECOMING A MOVIE STAR

Over the next few years, LL took a break from recording and focused heavily on his blossoming movie career. He accepted a high-profile role as a quick-witted but short-lived security guard in *Halloween H20: 20 Years Later*. He fared much better against a trio of intelligent sharks in *Deep Blue Sea*. His role as Sherman "Preacher" Dudley in the underwater thriller earned him the Blockbuster Entertainment Award for Favorite Supporting Actor in an Action Movie. He went on to appear in back-to-back blockbusters: Oliver Stone's football drama *Any Given Sunday*, and *Charlie's Angels*, opposite Cameron Diaz, Drew Barrymore, Lucy Liu, and Bill Murray. LL was quoted in the *Los Angeles Times* as saying that he was out to prove he was a real actor, not just someone "who can put butts in the seats." "I wanted to take [acting roles] seriously and not just be a celebrity stunt casting," he said. "I want to be able to deliver in whatever I do."

THE 2000s AND BEYOND

LL ushered in the new decade with a number of albums that wouldn't match the sales or accolades of his previous efforts. The first was *G.O.A.T.*, or the "Greatest of All Time." The album was LL's first to reach number one on the Billboard 200 chart when it debuted at the top spot. Despite its early success, the album's sales fizzled. His next album, *10*, was appropriately named to signify LL's tenth studio album. In the end, popular singles such as "Luv U Better," and the hit Jennifer Lopez duet, "All I Have," couldn't help *10* reach platinum status either. His 2004 album *The DEFinition* and 2006 self-titled LP *Todd Smith* also failed to go platinum. In July of 2006, LL announced that

(continues on page 85)

Once he had achieved success as a rapper, LL Cool J wanted to be taken seriously as an actor. LL has starred in many movies, including the critically acclaimed film *Any Given Sunday*, directed by Oliver Stone.

LL'S MOVIE CAREER

What started with a small cameo in *Krush Groove* has evolved into a full-fledged acting career. With more than 20 films under his belt and a few on the way, people may soon recognize LL more for his roles on the big screen than for his storied musical past. Here's a list of all the films in which LL has appeared:

Krush Groove (1985)
Wildcats (1986)
The Hard Way (1991)
Toys (1992)
Out-of-Sync (1995)
Touch (1997)
Caught Up (1998)
Woo (1998)
Halloween H20: 20 Years Later (1998)
Deep Blue Sea (1999)
In Too Deep (1999)
Any Given Sunday (1999)
Charlie's Angels (2000)
Kingdom Come (2001)
Rollerball (2002)
Deliver Us from Eva (2003)
S.W.A.T. (2003)
Mindhunters (2004)
Edison (2005)
Last Holiday (2006)
Heartland (2006)
Slow Burn (2007)

LL Cool J continues to expand his career, with the launch of the "Todd Smith" clothing line, geared towards a sophisticated and refined clientele. LL presented the Todd Smith clothing line at Olympus Fashion Week in New York City in 2006.

In 2006, LL Cool J co-authored the book *Platinum Workout* with his personal trainer, Dave Honig. The fitness book gives advice on how to achieve the perfect body, offering 5 phases of workouts, diet tips, and nutritional advice.

(continued from page 81)

he was planning to release the final album remaining on his contract with Def Jam, called *Todd Smith Pt. 2: Back to Cool*, in collaboration with fellow Queens rapper 50 Cent.

Along with his new album, LL focused on his "Todd Smith" clothing line, which catered to an upscale clientele, unlike most other hip-hop clothing designers that make casual clothes. "I would like a person to look rich, to look successful but not be overly ornate," LL told MSNBC.com at the launch of his line in February of 2006. "I want to leave room for the everyday guy to upgrade."

With a clothing line and two albums bearing his real name, LL Cool J finally introduced James Todd Smith to the world. Having tackled the hip-hop music scene, the fashion industry, the small screen, and the silver screen, LL Cool J is a multimedia superstar that will leave the world wondering just which bright horizon is next for him.

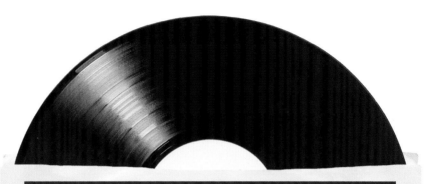

DISCOGRAPHY

Radio (1985)
Bigger and Deffer (1987)
Walking with a Panther (1989)
Mama Said Knock You Out (1990)
14 Shots to the Dome (1993)
Mr. Smith (1995)
All World: Greatest Hits (1996)
Phenomenon (1997)
G.O.A.T. (2000)
10 (2002)
The DEFinition (2004)
Todd Smith (2006)

▶ ▶▶ CHRONOLOGY ■ ‖

1968   **January 14** James Todd Smith born in Bay Shore, New York.

1972   Todd and Ondrea Smith move in with Ondrea's parents.

1973   Kool DJ Herc talks and rhymes over beat in the Bronx, New York, popularizing rap while working as a local DJ.

1979   Todd receives a turntable, microphone, mixer, and speakers from his grandfather. The Sugarhill Gang's recording "Rapper's Delight" brings hip-hop to the mass market. Todd attends a Sugarhill Gang concert held at the Harlem Armory in New York City.

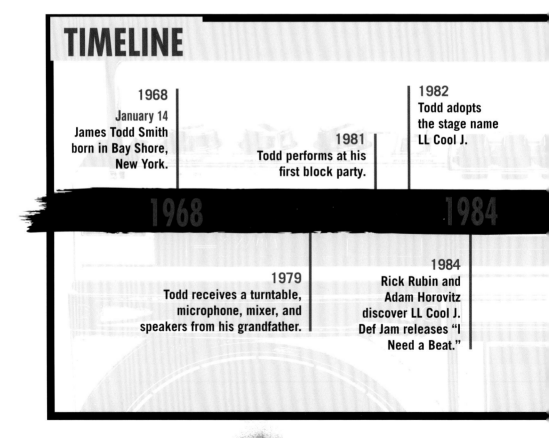

TIMELINE

1968
January 14
James Todd Smith
born in Bay Shore,
New York.

1981
Todd performs at his
first block party.

1982
Todd adopts
the stage name
LL Cool J.

1968

1984

1979
Todd receives a turntable,
microphone, mixer, and
speakers from his grandfather.

1984
Rick Rubin and
Adam Horovitz
discover LL Cool J.
Def Jam releases "I
Need a Beat."

1981   Todd performs at his first block party.

1982   Todd adopts the stage name LL Cool J.

1984   Rick Rubin and Adam Horovitz discover LL Cool J.
        Def Jam releases "I Need a Beat."

1985   LL Cool J has a cameo in the film *Krush Groove* and
        travels with the Fresh Fest Tour to learn showmanship
        from the tour's headliners Run DMC, the Fat Boys,
        and Whoodini.

1986   LL Cool J has his first gold single, "Rock the Bells."

1987   LL Cool J headlines the Def Jam Tour.

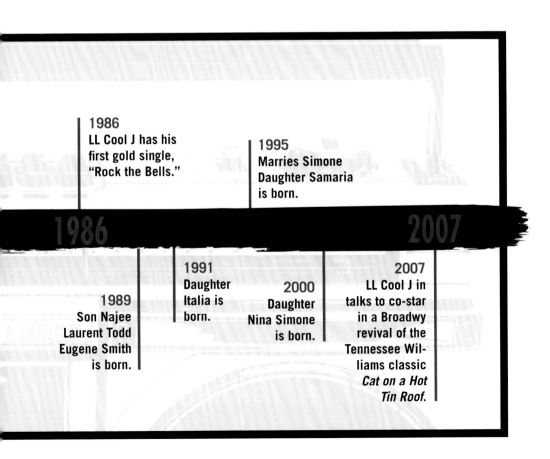

1986
**LL Cool J has his
first gold single,
"Rock the Bells."**

1995
**Marries Simone
Daughter Samaria
is born.**

1986   2007

1991
**Daughter
Italia is
born.**

1989
**Son Najee
Laurent Todd
Eugene Smith
is born.**

2000
**Daughter
Nina Simone
is born.**

2007
**LL Cool J in
talks to co-star
in a Broadwy
revival of the
Tennessee Wil-
liams classic
*Cat on a Hot
Tin Roof*.**

1988 Public Enemy releases *It Takes a Nation of Millions to Hold Us Back*, changing the direction of rap music.

1989 Son Najee Laurent Todd Eugene Smith is born.

1991 Daughter Italia is born.

1992 LL Cool J wins a Grammy Award for Best Rap Solo Performance and earns a role as Captain Patrick Zevo in the film *Toys*.

1993 LL Cool J performs at President Bill Clinton's inauguration.

1995 Marries Simone and has a role in the film *Out of Sync*. Daughter Samaria is born.

1998 LL Cool J writes and publishes his autobiography, *I Make My Own Rules*.

2000 Daughter Nina Simone is born.

2006 Launches James Todd Smith clothing line.

Releases fitness book *LL Cool J's Platinum Body*.

2007 LL Cool J in talks to co-star in a Broadway revival of the Tennessee Williams classic *Cat on a Hot Tin Roof*.

⏵⏵ GLOSSARY ⏹ ⏸

A&R Artist and repertoire (A&R) is a music industry term referring to the division of a record label responsible for scouting and developing talent. The A&R department is the link between the recording artist/act and the record label.

B-boy/B-girl Short for break boy and break girl; someone who break-dances.

backspinning Manually rotating a vinyl record in order to repeat key phrases or beats.

bling Expensive jewelry.

boroughs The five sections of New York City. The five boroughs are Queens, the Bronx, Manhattan, Brooklyn, and Staten Island.

break The most danceable part of a song, played over and over by DJs to keep the crowd dancing.

break beat The part of a dance song in which the singing stops but the percussion continues.

break dancing A dynamic, acrobatic style of dance.

crossover Expanding to a musical genre that is different from the one an artist is known for, usually resulting in a more mainstream popularity.

DJ Short for disc jockey; a hip-hop DJ (or spinner) creates the background music for rap songs by manipulating recordings through such techniques as audio mixing, scratching, and backspinning.

dozens Often considered a precursor of rap, the dozens is a word game dating back to the slave era in which one player taunts another by insulting or poking fun at his or her family.

gangsta rap Subculture of rap music focusing on street violence and gangsters.

graffiti   A form of street art in which "writers" use paint or permanent markers to make distinctive designs on the sides of subway cars, buildings, and other public and private surfaces.

griot   Linked by many scholars to modern rappers, the West African griot was a traveling troubadour who both educated and entertained his listeners with stories that were usually chanted in a rhythmic fashion.

hip-hop   A cultural movement that first developed in the predominantly African-American neighborhoods of the South Bronx during the 1970s and includes four elements: graffiti, break dancing, deejaying, and rap.

MC   A Master of Ceremonies (MC) is the host of a staged event. In the hip-hop world, rappers are called MCs.

posse   A group.

record label   A brand name created by companies that specialize in manufacturing, distributing, and promoting both audio and video recordings. The name derives from the paper label at the center of phonograph records (which have now been replaced by CDs).

sample   A small part of a recorded song that is used as part of the music for a new recorded song.

rap   A genre of music in which rhymed lyrics are spoken over rhythm tracks and snippets of recorded music and sounds.

remixes   Alternate mixes or arrangements of songs, usually for dance purposes.

rhythm and blues (R&B)   A style of African-American music that combines elements of blues and jazz and is usually performed with electric guitars and other electrically amplified instruments.

scratching   A deejay technique that results from the manual manipulation of a turntable to create a variety of sounds.

toasting   A Jamaican tradition in which the DJ at a dance party talks over songs; toasting was imported to the Bronx in the early seventies where it would play a key role in the development of rap.

turntables   The two record players sitting side by side that hip-hop DJs use to create the musical background for a rapper by mixing the records, scratching, and creating a beat.

BIBLIOGRAPHY

BOOKS

Chang, Jeff. *Can't Stop Won't Stop*. New York: St. Martin's Press, 2005.

Gueraseva, Stacy. *Def Jam, Inc.: Russell Simmons, Rick Rubin, and the Extraordinary Story of the World's Most Influential Hip-Hop Label*. New York: One World Books, 2005.

Smith, James Todd. *I Make My Own Rules*. New York: St. Martin's Press, 1998.

Edited by Alan Light. *The Vibe History of Hip Hop*. New York: Three Rivers Press, 1999.

MAGAZINES

Weisel, Al. "LL Cool J," *Rolling Stone* vol. 737 (Jun 1996): June 27, 1996.

WEB SITES

BBC News. "Run-DMC Quit after DJ Killing," BBC News. Available online. URL: *http://news.bbc.co.uk/2/hi/entertainment/2415565.stm*. Updated on November, 07, 2002.

David Browne. "LL Cool J: Walking with A Panther," Rolling Stone. Available online. URL: http://www.rollingstone.com/artists/llcoolj/albums/album/302087/review/6067477/walking_with_a_panther. Posted on September 7, 1989.

CNN. "Run-DMC Star, 37, Was Hip-hop Pioneer," CNN. Available online. URL: http://archives.cnn.com/2002/SHOWBIZ/Music/10/31/obit.jam.master.jay/. Updated on October, 31, 2002.

Cheo H Coker. "LL Cool J: Walking with A Panther," Rolling Stone. Available online. URL: http://www.rollingstone.com/artists/llcoolj/albums/album/323172/review/6067377/mr_smith. Posted on February 8, 1996.

Stephen Thomas Erlewine. "LL Cool J Bio," AOL Music. Available online. URL: *http://music.aol.com/artist/ll-cool-j/95754/biography*. Downloaded on September, 24, 2006.

Stephen Thomas Erlewine. "Raising Hell: Run-DMC," All Music Guide. Available online. URL: http://allmusic.com/cg/amg.dll?p=amg&sql=10:zr6m965o3ep6. Downloaded on September, 24, 2006

Steve Huey. "*Mamma Said Knock You Out* Review," All Music Guide. Available online. URL: *http://allmusic.com/cg/amg.dll?p=amg&sql=10:lj9ss38ba3rg*. Downloaded on September, 24, 2006.

Prairie Miller. "Interview with LL Cool J," NY Rock. Available online. URL: *http://www.nyrock.com/interviews/2001/llcoolj_int.asp*. Posted April, 2001.

Randy Reiss. "Canibus Says Feud with LL Cool J Was Poor Self-Promotion," VH1. Available online. URL: http://www.vh1.com/artists/news/502425/10081998/canibus.jhtml?partner=emailstoryfriend. Updated on October, 09, 1998.

▶ ▶ FURTHER READING ■ ||

Abrams, Dennis. *The Beastie Boys.* New York: Chelsea House, 2007.

Ayazi-Hashjin, Sherry. *Rap and Hip-Hop: The Voice of a Generation.* New York: Rosen Publishing, 1999.

Hoffman, Frank, general editor. *American Popular Music: Rhythm & Blues, Rap, and Hip-Hop.* New York: Facts on File, 2005.

Jones, Maurice K. *Say It Loud! The Story of Rap Music.* Minneapolis: Millbrook Press, 1994.

LL Cool J. *I Make My Own Rules.* New York: St. Martin's Press, 1998.

Lommel, Cookie. Russell Simmons. New York: Chelsea House, 2007.

Lommel, Cookie. *The History of Rap Music.* New York: Chelsea House, 2001.

Slavicek, Louise Chipley. *Run-DMC.* New York: Chelsea House, 2007.

Smith, James Todd. *I Make My Own Rules.* New York: St. Martin's Press, 1998.

PHOTO CREDITS

▸ ▸▸ INDEX ▪ ▐▐

▸ ▸▸ ABOUT THE AUTHORS ■ ❚❚

DUSTIN SHEKELL is a writer and music aficionado living in San Francisco. His birth and the genesis of rap music were separated by a matter of months, influencing him to bring linoleum to elementary school for break-dancing competitions during recess. To keep his breaking skills up to speed, he flattened cardboard boxes in the back of his dad's van to practice during long drives. He's known to do the Centipede to this day.

CHUCK D redefined rap music and hip-hop culture as leader and cofounder of legendary rap group Public Enemy. His messages addressed weighty issues about race, rage, and inequality with a jolting combination of intelligence and eloquence. A musician, writer, radio host, TV guest, college lecturer, and activist, he is the creator of Rapstation.com, a multiformat home on the Web for the vast global hip-hop community.